FACET BOOKS

HISTORICAL SERIES

F A C E T **fb** B O O K S

HISTORICAL SERIES — 5
(American Church)

Richard C. Wolf, Editor

The Protestant Quest
for a
Christian America
1830-1930

by ROBERT T. HANDY

FORTRESS PRESS   PHILADELPHIA

This study was first published as
"The Protestant Quest for a Christian America, 1830-1930"
in *Church History,* Vol. XXII, No. 1 (March, 1952), 8-20
(Published by The American Society of Church History, Berne, Ind.),
and is republished by arrangement with the publisher.

Published by Fortress Press, 1967
INTRODUCTION © 1967 BY FORTRESS PRESS
Library of Congress Catalog Card Number 67-22986

4081C67   Printed in U.S.A.   1-3041

Introduction

DURING the greater part of its history the United States has been, or has been considered, a "Protestant nation." In large measure this is due to the fact that the Spanish and French did not attempt to settle on the eastern seaboard area extending from what is now Maine to Georgia, thus leaving the territory which was to become the core of the emergent nation open for British and Protestant colonization.

The thirteen colonies were almost completely Protestant. Not only were the British colonists Protestant in either ecclesiastical affiliation or affinity; the continental-based immigrants were equally Protestant oriented. In 1785 there were probably fewer than twenty thousand Roman Catholics, nearly three-fourths of whom were concentrated in Maryland, among the 2,500,000 inhabitants of the new nation. Here and there a Roman Catholic such as Charles Carroll in Maryland wielded some influence in the struggle for independence and in the formation of the new nation, but in general the Roman Catholics had no great impact upon the life of the nation or upon its ecclesiastical and religious patterns. For the first quarter of its existence the United States was virtually monolithic in its Protestant orientation and character.

Beginning in the first quarter of the nineteenth century an incipient shift away from this monolithic Protestant structure can be observed. Massive waves of immigration brought a steadily mounting number of Roman Catholics to these shores, most of whom settled down in enclaves in the cities of the eastern and southern seaboard from Boston to New Orleans. A notable portion, however, moved into the mid-West with St. Louis as the center of their settlements. The unhappy story of the resistance to, rejection, and persecution of the growing Roman Catholic minority need not be treated here. It is sufficient to state that American Protestants took note of what they considered a threat to their political and religious supremacy and reacted in an unfortunately negative fashion.

In this same period more or less indigenous American religious groups sprang up. Antedating the period in their origins in America, the Methodists and Baptists became the leading groups in numerical membership in the United States between 1830 and the Civil War. In its own way each of these groups was an "American" ecclesiastical and religious movement. Prior to the Revolutionary War the Methodists in America had only a tenuous tie with the Wesleyans in England. Even before the War the southern Methodists, constituting the majority by 1776, were manifesting a marked tendency to try to go it on their own, even to the extent of proposing that they ordain their own clergy who could then administer the sacraments.

Such ordination would have terminated immediately the frustrating dependence upon Anglicans who, in general, had no liking for the Methodists. Shortly after the Revolutionary War the American Methodists, with the assistance of John Wesley, cut their ties with the Anglicans and emerged as a full-fledged ecclesiastical and spiritual organism in America. The Baptists tended to be even less closely related to their English counterparts than the Methodists. From their earliest days in Rhode Island the Baptists were notably American in their orientation and independent of support or control from abroad.

The first half of the nineteenth century saw the rise of American religious groups which did not have or did not claim any direct line of derivation from the Protestant Reformation. Some of these groups, such as the Shakers and a number of religious communisms of varying character, have disappeared. Others are very much present, for example the Disciples of Christ, the Church of Jesus Christ of the Latter Day Saints, the Unitarian-Universalist constellation, the United Brethren and the Evangelical Association (now the Evangelical United Brethren Church), the Adventist and Spiritualist groups, and others. Inroads were being made on the monolithic Protestant character of American Christianity.

Augmented immigration strengthened the Roman Catholic minority after the Civil War. Internecine strife wracked a number of the older Protestant groups, especially the Presbyterians and the Lutherans. Christian Science and the sect phenomenon appeared, draining strength from the old-line Protestant bodies. By the turn of the twentieth century the supremacy of the Protestant forces was under heavy attack and on the wane. When in 1928 the Democratic Party nominated a Roman Catholic, Alfred E. Smith, for the presidency the end of the Protestant era in the United States was clearly in sight. The end came in 1960 when John F. Kennedy was elected President without really serious resistance on religious grounds.

As the period of Protestant dominance drew to its close, students of the American religious scene began to give increasing attention to the transitions and shifts of power and influence which characterized the decline of the Protestant impact on and penetration of the American way of life. They have engaged in new, fresh, and sometimes novel interpretative approaches in their attempts to assay and evaluate the significance of the demise of the Protestant era both in terms of what is to be learned and in portents for the future.

Among those scholars who have made major contributions in the area of fresh interpretative efforts in American church history, especially in relation to the period since 1865, has been Robert T. Handy, Professor of Church History at Union Theological Seminary in New York. Professor Handy, following the lead of his illustrious mentor, Professor Sidney E. Mead, is a devoted exponent of the necessity of careful and penetrative study of the original source materials as the basis for experiments in interpretation of American church history. The years since 1865 have been the area of prime concentration for his study, with particular focus on twentieth-century American Protestantism.

The essay presented here is a broad-gauged interpretative treatment of the American religious scene between 1830 and 1930. This essay, along with an essay by Thomas T. McAvoy, *The Formation of the American Catholic Minority, 1820-1860,* should serve to provide a solid background for most of the other *FACET BOOKS—Historical Series* on American church history which are to follow. In its own right, however, and quite apart from any relationship to the remainder of the *FACET* series in American church history, the essay makes a valuable contribution to the understanding of the American religious scene in the mid-twentieth century.

On the basis of the broad terrain exposed in this study Professor Handy has, in subsequent studies, not only delved more deeply into particular areas, but together with H. Shelton Smith and Lefferts A. Loetscher has also engaged in a comprehensive study of the entire scene of American church history as understood through selected source documents bound together by a coordinating, interpretative account in the two-volume *American Christianity: An Historical Interpretation with Representative Documents* (New York: Charles Scribner's Sons, 1960, 1963). Narrowing his focus he has done a study of the cooperative home missions movement in *We Witness Together* (New York: Friendship Press, 1956). More recent research has produced a documentary work, *The Social Gospel in America, 1870-1920: Gladden, Ely, Rauschenbusch* (New York: Oxford University Press, 1966), and two articles: "The American Religious Depression, 1925-1935," Professor Handy's presidential address to the American Society of Church History, in *Church History,* XXIX (1960), 3-16; and "The American Tradition of Religious Liberty: An Historical Analysis," in the *Journal of Public Law,* XIII (1964), 247-266. Professor Handy also wrote the chapter entitled "The American Scene" in *Twentieth Century Christianity,* edited by Stephen Neill (London: Collins, 1961, reprinted in the United States by Dolphin Books, 1963).

After ordination to the Baptist ministry in 1943, Professor Handy was pastor of a congregation in Illinois and a chaplain with the Army. He received his Ph.D. degree from the Divinity School of the University of Chicago in 1949, and joined the faculty of Union Theological Seminary in 1950, where he has been Professor of Church History since 1959.

RICHARD C. WOLF

The Divinity School
Vanderbilt University
Nashville, Tennessee
June, 1967

THE PROTESTANT QUEST FOR A
CHRISTIAN AMERICA
1830-1930

AMERICAN Christianity is so diversified and confusing and its material is of such vast extent that the scholars who have worked at the broader aspects of its history have had to bring to their study certain interpretative theses in order to find their way through the material at all.[1] These interpretative theses, some implicitly held and others explicitly stated, some relatively adequate and others fairly weak, have paved the way for a great deal of intensive research, so that the young discipline of American church history has a solid and illuminating body of material. Out of the research thus far undertaken have sprung new themes of interpretation, putting into operation what may be called an "historiographical cycle." This interaction of research and interpretation has functioned sufficiently well enough that the overall picture of American Christian history grows steadily clearer. The process of

[1] I am greatly indebted to Professor Sidney E. Mead, in whose seminars the matters dealt with in this paper were confronted, for stimulating suggestions, illuminating references, and constant encouragement.

1

clarification has, however, proceeded satisfactorily only to a point—to the Civil War. For the years since the Civil War, the picture has not yet come into sharp focus.[2] The interpretative theses thus far proposed have had serious limitations, and as a result the "historiographical cycle" has not operated to best advantage. The excellent monographic studies that have been made remain, therefore, somewhat unrelated and leave us with a rather fragmentary understanding of religious history since 1865. Yet in these years occurred decisive developments which must be further probed and clarified if we are to understand more fully the contemporary American religious scene, now so important a part of the total life of the world church. To be sure, most of the significant movements of the period have received some attention, but they can be fully understood and their significance grasped only as they are delineated as part of the total history of American Christianity with the interconnections traced and the polarities analyzed. More fruitful and better-directed monographic studies will follow from the setting forth of fresh and rounded themes of interpretation; the "historiographical cycle" will then operate to better advantage for this important period.

It is not difficult to explain why general overall

[2] It is customary in the periodization of American history to date a new period from 1865. As far as *church* history is concerned, the basic similarity of the Protestant pattern before and after 1865 suggests that a preferable periodization is 1830-1930, with a possible sub-division in 1890. The latter two thirds of this period now needs particular attention.

2

interpretations of accepted adequacy have not yet appeared. Professor Cyril C. Richardson has reminded us that "Church History is the tale of redemption; and while in a sense it embraces world history, its central thread is the story of the Holy Community (known under various guises and found in manifold and surprising places), which is the bearer of revelation and through which God acts in human history."[3] And Professor James Hastings Nichols has noted that the gift of the church historian "is not for abstractions, but for penetration and interpretation and ordering of the concrete."[4] But to penetrate and interpret and order the concrete, when that concrete is the Holy Community which in America is known under extremely various guises and found in most manifold and unbelievably surprising places, is a task which we would eschew were it not so vital.

The task is even more difficult for the years since the 1860's, for a whole culture was passing in those fateful years of civil strife. A strange new world emerged as Lincoln's successors took up their duties, a strange new world that provided a changed and perplexing milieu for the Christian church. The most expressive comment regarding the profound transformations of post-Civil War America was made by Henry Adams:

[3] "Church History Past and Present," *Union Seminary Quarterly Review,* V (November, 1949), 13.

[4] "The Art of Church History," *Church History,* XX (March, 1951), 9.

3

My country in 1900 is something totally different from my own country in 1860: I am wholly a stranger in it. Neither I, nor anyone else, understands it. The turning of a nebula into a star may somewhat resemble the change. All I can see is that it is one of compression, and consequent development of terrific energy, represented not by souls, but by coal and iron and steam.[5]

The difficulty of dealing with the church history of such a time in any full-orbed way is evident; the difficulty is in some ways heightened by the very richness of source materials: books, sermons, periodicals, yearbooks, catalogs, pamphlets, tracts, newspapers, not to mention the archives of the denominations, the great societies, and the interdenominational agencies. But despite the difficulties, there is need for fresh and comprehensive overall views or themes of interpretation to guide and direct the study of recent American church history.

The views proposed a generation ago by Professor Henry Kalloch Rowe would today find favor in but few quarters. He suggested that the history of religion in America is the history of emancipation, emancipation successively from the authority of a state church, from the formal worship and preaching of the earlier divines, and from the traditional ideas of a Protestant

[5] *Letters, 1892-1918*, p. 279, quoted in Henry Steele Commager, *The American Mind: An Interpretation of American Thought and Character Since the 1880's* (New Haven: Yale University Press, 1950), pp. 134 f.

orthodoxy. In this broad setting, he treated the period since the Civil War under the topics "Rationalizing Religion," "Socializing Religion," and "Spiritualizing Religion."[6] This approach ignored large ranges of Christian life and thought, and viewed the rest through the narrow focus of one viewpoint. The dean of American church historians, William Warren Sweet, has focused his work mainly on pre-Civil War periods. His arduous research, his most useful interpretative themes, and the bulk of his writings are devoted to the generations before 1860.

Professor Arthur M. Schlesinger, Sr. has given the clearest statement of a significant and fruitful approach to the recent period, an approach that has guided a great deal of research. In an article entitled "A Critical Period in American Religion, 1875-1900,"[7] Dr. Schlesinger advanced the fertile thesis that during the last quarter of the nineteenth century organized religion in America faced two great challenges—the one to its system of thought, the other to its social program. A rather important series of studies of Protestantism have followed this general approach.[8] These studies have

[6] *The History of Religion in the United States* (New York: Macmillan, 1924), pp. vii f.

[7] *Massachusetts Historical Society Proceedings,* LXIV (June, 1932), 523-47, republished in *Facet Books—Historical Series* (Philadelphia: Fortress Press, 1967).

[8] E.g., Aaron Ignatius Abell, *The Urban Impact on American Protestantism 1865-1900* (Cambridge: Harvard University Press, 1943); B. J. Loewenberg, "Darwinism Comes to America," *Mississippi Valley Historical Review,* XXVIII (1941), 339-68; Henry F. May, *Protestant Churches and Industrial America* (New York: Harper & Bros., 1949).

their limitations, however. They focus attention on the North and the East, on the great cities, on the seminary centers, and on the denominational and interdenominational headquarters, while they practically ignore important geographical areas and scarcely notice some large households of faith. An even more serious limitation of this approach is that in utilizing the biological analogy of stimulus-response it is easy to slip into the notion that Christianity was a static entity which, after being confronted with this or that external challenge, after a greater or lesser time responded with more or less adequacy. This can lead to a vastly oversimplified view of what the American churches were and contribute to a serious underrating of the inner drive and dynamic of the churches. Furthermore, this approach enables the researcher to study the churches in terms of criteria which he has drawn from some other source than a consideration of what the churches consider to be their main task and role in society. This may be a perfectly legitimate undertaking, but it is not the primary role of the church historian.

I would like to put forward in an exploratory way a view which is in many respects somewhat the reverse of the stimulus-response thesis. The Protestantism that faced post-Civil War America was far from being a static entity continually being challenged by external forces. Rather it was an aggressive, dynamic form of Christianity that set out confidently to confront American life at every level, to permeate, evangelize, and

Christianize it. The results of this Protestant thrust were ambivalent: on the one hand there were some notable achievements, but on the other there was an entanglement and partial envelopment by an increasingly pluralistic and secularized culture.

The middle third of the nineteenth century, roughly the years 1830-1860, was a period in which conservative, sectarian, evangelical Protestantism was a dominant force on the American scene. The French observer de Tocqueville remarked that "in the United States the sovereign authority is religious and consequently hypocrisy must be common; but there is no country in the world where the Christian religion retains a greater influence over the souls of men than in America. . . ."[9] A domestic observer, Robert Baird, gave evidence repeatedly in his massive study of the vast hold of the evangelical churches on American life.[10] Recent study has underlined how important the traditional faith and morality of Protestantism was as a force in pre-Civil War America. The attempt to understand the cataclysm of the Civil War itself leads directly to a consideration of the anti-slavery movement which grew out of and was stamped with the pattern of pietistic Protestantism. Analyses of the national faith in democracy point to the decisive sway of Christian ideas; Professor Ralph H. Gabriel notes

[9] Alexis de Tocqueville, *Democracy in America* (New York: Alfred A. Knopf, 1945) I, 303.

[10] *Religion in America* (New York: Harper & Bros., 1856), esp. pp. 536 ff., 586 f., 658 ff.

7

that "the foundation of this democratic faith was a frank supernaturalism derived from Christianity. The twentieth-century student is often astonished at the extent to which supernaturalism permeated American thought of the nineteenth century."[11] The cultural dominance of Protestantism was illustrated in the transition to a public tax-supported school system. This transition was palatable to Protestants because the schools were rather clearly Protestant in orientation, though "non-sectarian." Protestant cultural leadership was reflected in the realm of higher education also— as a report in 1857 stated it, "We might go through the whole list of American colleges, and show that, with here and there an exception, they were founded by religious men, and mainly with an eye to the interests of the Church."[12] Historians whose major interests are not religious sometimes react with some surprise when they are forced to recognize how widespread Protestant influence was in the first part of the nineteenth century. Professor Whitney R. Cross, for example, in his recent and useful work, *The Burned-over District,* records how widespread the circulation of religious journals was in the first part of the nineteenth century and how avidly they were read. He comments, "Now that theology is a very nearly dead subject, one finds it extremely difficult to realize how

11 *The Course of American Democratic Thought: An Intellectual History Since 1815* (New York: The Ronald Press Co., 1940), p. 14.

12 Quoted by Donald G. Tewksbury in *The Founding of American Colleges and Universities Before the Civil War* (New York: Teachers' College, 1932), p. 56.

such journals could have an extensive appeal. But appeal they did, in demonstrable fashion."[13] Then he seeks to explain this appeal:

The puzzle of such an attraction resolves itself in two ways. First, a continuing itineracy often accompanied the paper, making local friends who in turn urged its support. A train of camp meetings, revivals, conventions, and quarterly sessions also kept adherents in contact. To others beyond immediate reach, the magazine, even were its heavy doses of theology not read, could be a constant reminder of intellectual and spiritual ties, while some leisurely seepage of doctrine originally imbibed by ear might filter into the inner consciousness. But suggestion of such indirect influence begs the major question. It seems an inescapable conclusion that a considerable proportion even of laymen read and relished the theological treatises.[14]

The great revivals of 1857-59 provide further evidence of the power and prestige of evangelical Protestantism; a recent student of the revivals has noted that "there was remarkable unanimity of approval among religious and secular observers alike, with scarcely a critical voice heard anywhere."[15] There

[13] *The Burned-over District: The Social and Intellectual History of Enthusiastic Religion in Western New York, 1800-1850* (Ithaca: Cornell University Press, 1950), p. 108.

[14] *Ibid.*, pp. 108 f.

[15] J. Edwin Orr, *The Second Evangelical Awakening in Britain* (London: Marshall, Morgan & Scott, Ltd., 1949), p. 21.

9

were, of course, Protestant groups whose interpretation of Christianity was not that of the conservative evangelicals, but they were small in comparison. The latter dominated the religious press, which had grown more than had the secular press in the twenty years before 1865, both in number of periodicals and in circulation.[16] Protestantism was fully committed to and profited from the principle of religious liberty and the voluntary method in religion, anticipating continued progress on this basis. Finally, orthodox Protestantism had grown up with the individualism that characterized nineteenth-century America, had contributed to its rise, and found it thoroughly congenial. In the words of Henry May, "Organized Protestantism supported the dominant economic beliefs and institutions even more unanimously than it accepted the existing form of government."[17] In many ways, the middle third of the nineteenth century was more of a "Protestant Age" than was the colonial period with its established churches.

At the close of the Civil War there were approximately five million Protestant church members out of an estimated population of some thirty-two million. Protestantism's influence, of course, extended far beyond its actual membership; the vast majority of Americans were encompassed in "popular" if not in "ecclesi-

[16] Winfred Ernest Garrison, *The March of Faith: The Story of Religion in America Since 1865* (New York: Harper & Bros., 1933), p. 10.

[17] May, *op. cit.*, p. 6.

astical" Protestantism.[18] The Protestants were an aggressive, self-confident, and surprisingly homogeneous group. To be sure, they were divided into denominations among which considerable tension could arise, yet there was a fundamental similarity. De Tocqueville stated that "they all differ in respect to the worship which is due to the Creator; but they all agree in respect to the duties which are due from man to man. Each sect adores the Deity in its own peculiar manner, but all sects preach the same moral law in the name of God."[19] As the denominations faced their country they saw no reason why their influence should not continue to grow and their numbers increase, and they set out to evangelize and Christianize every aspect of American life. Their tremendous drive scattered churches across the West; church extension and church building were major focal points of Protestant concern throughout the nineteenth century. The restless energy of expanding Protestantism made possible the steady growth of the denominations and the erection of elaborate denominational structures. The inner dynamic of Protestantism led to the extension of existing cooperative agencies and societies as well as the development of many new ones devoted to the promotion of revivals, the advancement of good causes, the furtherance of education, and the expansion of missions, home

[18] H. Paul Douglass, "Religion—The Protestant Faiths," in Harold E. Stearns (ed.), *America Now: An Inquiry into Civilization in the United States* (New York: Charles Scribner's Sons, 1938), pp. 505-27.

[19] De Tocqueville, *op. cit.*, I, 303.

11

and foreign. The desire to permeate the life of America with the leaven of Christianity led to the adoption and imaginative use of such new instruments as the Y.M.C.A.[20] This religious drive to Christianize the nation was a phase of the energy that characterized American life in general at that time, but the evangelical fervor of the Protestant denominations intensified it.

As Protestantism set about the task of permeating and Christianizing American life, the very seriousness of the effort magnified the tendency of churches to absorb the characteristics of those whom they served. The culture they were trying to Christianize grew steadily less homogeneous after the Civil War. The horrors of reconstruction widened the chasm between South and North; the great denominations of those sections, striving to reach every level of their respective sections, identified themselves warmly with their people and the broken spiritual ties were not healed. In the North and East particularly, the impact of evolutionary and historical thinking began to upset many, especially those of the educated classes. Their churches came to feel the obligation to understand the new conditions and mediate the gospel to such folk. Henry Ward Beecher, whose genius apparently lay largely in his ability to express to perfection what his huge congregations were thinking, declared: "The providence

[20] Cf. C. Howard Hopkins, *History of the Y.M.C.A. in North America* (New York: Association Press, 1951).

of God is rallying forward a spirit of investigation that Christian ministers must meet and join. There is no class of people upon earth who can less afford to let the development of truth run ahead of them than they."[21] Ministers who moved in the circles where such currents were flowing tried to stand between the new modes of thought and the old theology; it was from among the ardent evangelicals that the liberal pioneers came. The full secularity to which the new ways of thinking could run was not then clear, and the older theology was often expressed in intransigent and stylized forms that repelled Christians sensitive to the needs of their day. Hence "liberalism" arose not so much from outside as from within, as prominent evangelicals seeking to live out their faith moved among people troubled by new intellectual trends.[22] In the major denominations of the North particularly, the liberal trend was evident in the late nineteenth century, at times painfully evident.

A great deal of Protestant America, of course, lived in rural and small town areas where the new winds blew faintly, and where the cyclones of the cultural centers had warned the faithful to erect storm signals.

[21] Ernest Trice Thompson, *Changing Emphases in American Preaching* (Philadelphia: Westminster Press, 1943), p. 86.

[22] Cf. Daniel Day Williams, *The Andover Liberals: A Study in American Theology* (New York: King's Crown Press, 1941); cf. also George Hammar, *Christian Realism in Contemporary American Theology* (Uppsala: A. B. Lundequistska Bokhandeln, 1940), especially the note on p. 153, where he stresses the evangelical center of Rauschenbusch's liberal theology.

Hence the same post-Civil War years that are marked by the leftward trend are also characterized by the rightward movement of a counter-reformation which was rooted in the conservative, evangelical, revivalistic Protestantism of the earlier nineteenth century, but showing a hardening and a narrowing of that tradition. Again, we see Protestant zeal at work. We see the Protestant churches identifying themselves with the concerns of the people, matching themselves to their level. The conservative reaction was of course by no means limited to the small town and rural areas; it swept into the great urban centers where city conditions were severing people from their cultural roots and where many of the city masses had a longing for the religious securities of their rural youth. An early dramatic expression of the conservative reaction was a hugely attended Prophetic Conference in New York in 1877, followed by one eight years later in Chicago. At these conferences the liberal drifts and compromises made with the world were deplored; the prophetic and premillennial doctrines were vigorously proclaimed. The rightward trend was strengthened by the appeal to the authority of the infallible Bible. This stream of conservative thought was especially evident in the great Bible conferences: Niagara, Winona, Rocky Mountain. The conservative trend was supported and carried both to the greatest cities and the tiniest hamlets of America by the host of revivalists of the late nineteenth and early twentieth centuries. One student of

14

revivalism, writing twenty-five years ago, noted that "if collected in one volume with only a paragraph apiece, the revivalists of the last fifty years would form a book that would dwarf an unabridged dictionary."[23]

The denominations were thus the locus of both leftward and rightward movements; they lost a great deal of inner unity and suffered sharp inner tensions, climaxed by the fundamentalist-modernist controversy of the 1920's. The "institutionalists" had their tasks cut out for them in reconciling the tension between "fundamentalists" and "experimentalists."[24] That they were as successful as they were is a tribute to their skill and tenacity in a day when churches of the same denomination a block or two apart could be moving in opposite directions. Yet even in those stormy years the contending parties were far more alike than unlike. Though their definitions of Christianity differed, still they were one in their effort to Christianize a nation, and this essentially missionary task was perhaps what held the denominations together. In 1912 Professor David S. Schaff wrote an article entitled "The Movement and Mission of American Christianity." It is significant to observe on what grounds his defense of the separation of church and state and the voluntary system in religion rests: "It is for the American church to

[23] Grover C. Loud, *Evangelized America* (New York: Dial Press, 1928), p. 257.

[24] Terminology used by Kirsopp Lake; cf. Gaius Glenn Atkins, *Religion in Our Times* (New York: Round Table Press, 1932), p. 219.

15

show that the claim made for it is true, that it is the Scriptural method and is best adapted to develop Christian manhood, and to permeate society with the leaven of the Christian religion."[25] To permeate society with the leaven of the Christian religion—this was the focus of Protestant energy and a source of Protestant unity despite diversity and tension.

The Christian social movements which arose in the years after the Civil War shared in the Protestant quest for a Christian America; their attention was focused on the economic, social, and political aspects of the nation's life, where revolutionary transformations were going on.

With the commitment to a philosophy of individualism that was so strongly evident in nineteenth-century Protestantism, adjustment was more difficult for Protestantism in this sphere than in some others, and the challenge-response thesis has had its widest and most valid application precisely at this point.[26] Some within the church, particularly where liberalism had paved the way, were prepared to move more swiftly and more deeply into this field than others, yet the Christian social movement was not limited to the social gospel of the evangelical liberals—there was also an American Christian Commission, a Salvation Army, a rescue mission movement. In these movements both evangeli-

[25] *American Journal of Theology,* XVI (January, 1912), 65.
[26] Note especially the cautious use of it in C. Howard Hopkins, *The Rise of the Social Gospel in American Protestantism 1865-1915* ("Yale Studies in Religious Education," Vol. XIV [New Haven: Yale University Press, 1940]).

cal fervor and the drive to Christianize social relations are evident. *In His Steps*[27] reads quite differently from *Christianizing the Social Order*,[28] but they were both powerful expressions of a similar fundamental motif. There were crucial differences in theology and social philosophy between social gospel and conservative Protestants, but both groups strove to make America Christian. The Christian social movement was not only a response to external pressure; it was also a redirection, varied and often slow and cautious, of the inner vitality of Protestantism. Hence even at the point of its greatest validity, the challenge-response view must be used with care.

Despite its zeal and energy, Protestantism's dominance in culture and education, so evident at the mid-nineteenth-century mark, had ebbed by the 1920's. Many who had come from Protestant backgrounds had become estranged from the church or grown indifferent to it; secularization was clearly on the increase. Protestant thought, especially in certain liberal circles, was showing the effect of culture, more than the reverse.[29] The racial, sectional, and class lines that were still drawn within Protestantism suggest rather disturbingly that the Protestant effort to permeate and Christianize society had not had too profound an effect even on

27 [Charles M. Sheldon, *In His Steps* (Philadelphia, Chicago: John C. Winston Company, 1937).—ED.]

28 [Walter Rauschenbusch, *Christianizing the Social Order* (New York: Macmillan Company, 1942).—ED.]

29 Cf. Arnold Nash (ed.), *Protestant Thought in the Twentieth Century* (New York: Macmillan, 1951).

its own social fabric. The tide, flowing strongly in
Protestant favor in mid-nineteenth century, had clearly
turned by the third decade of the twentieth century.
At least part of the complex reasons for this can be
seen in the operation of sociological forces which
changed the structure of both Protestantism and the
society in which it moved, and which diluted and dulled
the Protestant thrust. Professor Leonard J. Trinterud
has recently observed that American church historians
are not making a serious attempt at a church history
for America because "most students of American
Christianity have adopted the sociological approach,
and thus—in strict definition—they have changed
fields. They have become historians of the sociological
phenomena of religion in American culture."[30] No
doubt Dr. Trinterud is pointing out that the church
historian has a distinctive task that he alone can under-
take. But in the attempt to clarify the religious history
of the age that saw the rise of sociology in the effort
to understand itself, to fail to use that discipline where
it is relevant would be pedantry indeed. Dr. H. Paul
Douglass has described the increase of the associative
over the community aspects of American life in the
period since the Civil War in a most illuminating
way. The Protestant dominance in the early nineteenth
century he finds to be "a triumph of religion still on
the communal level."[31] But with the rapid urbaniza-

[30] "Some Notes on Recent Periodical Literature on Colonial American Church History," *Church History,* XX (December, 1951), 73.

[31] Douglass, *loc. cit.,* p. 514.

tion that took place thereafter, the groupings of society became steadily less community-centered and more and more associative in nature, forming voluntarily around single interests. This has meant that

> the church tends to get reduced merely to one of the many groups in which persons, detached from locality, associate together with segments of their personalities. Moreover, each segment of personality, expressing itself in a different context and as a response to a different set of people, tends to project a separate set of moral standards. In this segmentation of culture we find the essence of urbanization, and, as well, the substitution of multiple moral standards for a single communal standard.[32]

Urbanization in both its rural and city phases has thus brought the church what Douglass goes so far as to call "the greatest inner revolution it has ever known." In effect, the church was in part remolded on the associative principle in the face of a segmented, pluralistic, associative culture. By this culture the Protestant thrust was diluted, blunted, absorbed. Though the churches, with their characteristic strengths and weaknesses and their varying definitions of themselves, strove zealously to penetrate and permeate American life, their impact was in some measure fragmented and disrupted by the nature of the society in which they worked. All this helps us to understand why Protestantism lost ground,

[32] *Ibid.*, p. 515.

why cults and sects have mushroomed since the Civil War, why denominations have often limited their ministrations to a given racial or nationality group, why local churches have often served a particular community interest. The associative nature of society in combination with the tendency of churches to identify themselves with the interests of the folk they serve contributed to the peculiar situation of American Protestantism, whereby the churches became entangled in cultural, racial, and class barriers instead of transcending them. Protestantism hoped to permeate and Christianize a society, but was instead partly enveloped by it.

Consideration of the weaknesses and difficulties of Protestantism in an associative culture, however, must not blind us to major institutional advances achieved by Protestant churches in the years since Appomattox. The percentage of Protestant church membership in the total population more than doubled, and in a time when the general population had tripled—no small achievement. Protestantism slightly more than kept pace with the remarkable rise in the level of wealth, and though this brought certain dangers, it testifies to denominational energy. Protestant zeal did not flag in those years; Professor Gaius Glenn Atkins has declared:

The first fifteen years of the twentieth century may sometime be remembered in America as the Age of Crusades. There were a superabundance of zeal,

a sufficience of good causes, unusual moral idealism,
excessive confidence in mass movements and leaders
with rare gifts of popular appeal. . . . Twentieth
century church crusades were also a continuation in
social, moral and even political regions, of nineteenth century evangelism.[33]

With somewhat diminishing force, this pattern continued throughout the 1920's. Protestant organizations
grew steadily more extensive and complex as they dealt
with the problems of the new age—to be sure the rise
of denominational bureaucracy was an ambiguous bless-
ing, but it reveals inner vitality. Though denominations
were strained by theological tension and schisms re-
sulted, major disruptions were avoided and unitive
tendencies within denominations and denominational
families operated even more strongly as the years
passed. Extensive home and foreign missionary activi-
ties were sustained throughout. Protestant vitality produced significant movements toward comity and coop-
eration, signalized in the establishment of the Federal
Council of the Churches of Christ in America in 1908
and in the formation of a number of other cooperative
organizations. Counter-tendencies against cultural envelopment were at work; they have flowered in our
own day in the theological revival and the ecumenical
movement. On the institutional level the years since
the Civil War were years of remarkable achievement.
On the intellectual level such a case cannot be made;

[33] Atkins, *op. cit.*, pp. 156 f.

conservatives tended to defend their tradition in a somewhat uncreative and external way while liberals were so enamoured with modern thought that they were in danger of surrendering too much of their tradition.

The history of Roman Catholicism in the same period offers some substantiation for the view that in the years since the Civil War an aggressive Protestantism hoped to strengthen further the position she had won in the middle third of the nineteenth century and further permeate American life, and that the result was remarkable achievement and yet an entanglement and partial envelopment by a culture increasingly associative in nature. Roman Catholicism in 1865 claimed three million adherents—by far the largest single religious group. It had been the church of the lower class, the immigrant, the city worker, and formed a religious enclave in Protestant America, a despised minority group for the most part. In the post-Civil War years a new spirit began to sweep through Catholicism. Henceforth it was to be less apologetic, less concerned with mere survival and more with consolidation and naturalization. It began to dream of permeating American life and remaking it in its image.

These new motifs were evident at the meeting of the Second Plenary Council at Baltimore in 1866, where it was noted with enthusiasm that the number of churches and clergy had doubled since the First Plenary fourteen years before. The convert Father Isaac Hecker gave clear expression to the new hope of Catholics when in 1868 he suggested that perhaps by 1900 the majority of Americans would be Catholic. He announced as his avowed purpose not only to "Catholicize America" but also to "Americanize Catholicism."[34] In 1868 James Gibbons (1834-1921) was consecrated bishop, and he is so much the symbol of the Roman Catholicism of his time that those years can be styled "the age of Gibbons." His desire to make the church at home in America, to naturalize the church, to identify her more closely with the life of America is evident in a remark he made about his popular book, *Faith of Our Fathers:*

> Of all things about the book, the point that gratifies me most is that, although it is an explanation of the Catholic religion, there is not one word in it that can give offence to our Protestant brethren. There was originally a reference that seemed to displease Episcopalians, but when my attention was called to it, I ordered it to be expunged.[35]

Archbishop John Ireland was another prelate who expressed a dominant mood of the American Catholicism of the half-century after the Civil War. He once said, preaching before a Catholic conference:

> It will not do to understand the thirteenth century

---

[34] [Quoted from Winfred E. Garrison, *The March of Faith* (New York: Harper & Brothers, 1933), p. 200. Cf. Walter Elliott, *Life of Father Hecker* (New York: Catholic Book Exchange, 1888).—ED.]

[35] Will, *Gibbons,* II, 886 f., quoted by Theodore Maynard, *The Story of American Catholicism* (New York: Macmillan, 1941).

better than the nineteenth. . . . We should speak to
our age; we should be in it, and of it, if we would
have its ear. For the same reason there is needed a
thorough sympathy with the country. The Church
of America must be, of course, as Catholic as even
in Jerusalem or Rome; but as far as her garments
assume colour from the local landscape, she must be
American.[36]

Here is evident the operation of the desire to permeate
society and to this end to identify the church with it
to a certain extent, the same concern we have seen in
operation in Protestantism.

In the case of Catholicism with its authoritarian
structure, the counter-tendencies could act more swiftly.
The decision of the Third Plenary Council of 1884 to
develop a parochial school system on a large scale is
one evidence of this. The resistance of Europe to
"Americanization," symbolized by Leo XIII's Apostolic
Letter, *Testem Benevolentiae,*[37] to Cardinal Gibbons in
1899, checked the drift to a yet more distinctive American Catholicism and pointed to the end of the era of
fraternization. Through all of this half-century, to be
sure, the church had to struggle hard against the disruptive tendencies of particular national groups in her
membership; in some areas the church was so iden-

[36] Willard L. Sperry, *Religion in America* (New York: Macmillan,
1946), p. 219.

[37] [Papal letter to James Cardinal Gibbons, January 22, 1899, in
Acta Sanctae Sedis (Rome: 1865 f.), Vol. 31 (1898/99), 471 ff. Cf.
John J. Wynne (ed.), *The Great Encyclical Letters of Pope Leo XIII*
(New York: Benziger, 1903).—ED.]

tified with the interests of particular enclaves of immigrants that there was serious inner conflict. In Cahenslyism (1891)[38] the disruptive tendencies of our associative, pluralistc culture had their impact in Catholicism, but they were resisted, and the foundation of present Catholic strength was cemented.

In conclusion, I want to underline the importance of this period for the Protestant church historian. For the Protestantism of the period, despite its zeal, exhibited a certain negativeness that we are seeking to escape today; the zeal was often exercised in a negative setting, directed against something. Liberalism certainly had its share of negative elements; the conservative reaction also was often far more powerful in denunciation than in affirmation. And even in charitable judgment, it is hard to avoid a certain superficiality in a Protestantism that became so entangled in cultural patterns.

Our generation should repeat these charges of negativeness and superficiality with hesitation, keeping in mind Professor H. Richard Niebuhr's warning that "the evil habit of men in all times to criticize their predecessors for having seen only half of the truth hides from them their own partiality and incompleteness."[39]

[38] [The movement's name is derived from the name of its leader, Peter Cahensly, who proposed that the parish system of the Roman Catholic Church in the United States be organized along ethnic lines, thus perpetuating nationalistic barriers, and thereby retarding the orientation of the Roman Catholic immigrants into the American scene.—ED.]

[39] *The Kingdom of God in America* (Chicago: Willett, Clark & Co., 1937), p. xiii.

But because of the negativeness and superficiality there may be a tendency to brush the period aside as a time of deviation from classical Protestantism which can serve mainly as a warning to us. The significance of the period is far deeper. It was then that the churches came face to face with the confused, troubled, fragmented, pluralistic, unstable new world of science and technology.

This first period of engagement with the kind of problems American churches are likely to be faced with for some time to come teaches lessons which are important in their positive as well as their negative aspects. The achievements of that period provide much of the religious capital on which we still draw. The tensions that arose then have not entirely been resolved; historical study of these tensions can help us to keep them from becoming destructive again. Many of the patterns of secularization that today keep men from a vital relationship to the Christian faith were developed and applied in this period. Professor Sidney E. Mead has suggested that the "secular" mind of today is to be saved by a

return to God, and that this in turn can be furthered by stimulating him to remember his true antecedents —his true self. . . . This is to say that the so-called "secularized" man of today, inside or outside of a church, is really indebted to the Christian tradition for the insights regarding human nature and destiny upon which he builds his structure of hope and aspiration—but that he is largely unaware of his indebtedness.[40]

A profound knowledge of the religious history of the years since the Civil War can be useful in approaching such people, some of whom can be guided to see that the values they treasure are products of the Christian faith, and cannot be maintained for long apart from positive Christianity. Finally, in many important respects the church was carrying out its redemptive work on several frontiers, geographical, social, ecumenical—and as it appears that in the discernible future the church will sojourn in an alien world, surely the history of the work of the churches of Christ in that time of frontiers is highly significant.

[40] "The Task of the Church Historian," *The Chronicle*, XII (July, 1949), 139. Cf. John Baillie, *Invitation to Pilgrimage* (New York: Charles Scribner's Sons, 1942).

27

For Further Reading

RICHARDSON, CYRIL C. "Church History Past and Present," in *Union Theological Seminary Review,* November, 1949.

COMMAGER, HENRY STEELE. *The American Mind: An Interpretation of American Thought and Character Since the 1880's.* New Haven: Yale University Press, 1950.

ABELL, AARON I. *The Urban Impact on American Protestantism, 1865-1900.* Cambridge: Harvard University Press, 1943.

TOCQUEVILLE, ALEXIS DE. *Democracy in America.* New York: Alfred A. Knopf, 1945.

GABRIEL, RALPH H. *The Course of American Democratic Thought: An Intellectual History Since 1815.* New York: The Ronald Press, 1940.

MAY, HENRY F. *Protestant Churches and Industrial America.* New York: Harper & Bros., 1949.

GARRISON, WINFRED ERNEST. *The March of Faith: The Story of Religion in America Since 1865.* New York: Harper & Bros., 1933.

DOUGLASS, H. PAUL, "Religion—The Protestant Faiths," in *America Now: An Inquiry Into Civilization in the United States.* Edited by Harold E. Stearns. New York: Charles Scribner's Sons, 1938. Pages 505-527.

NIEBUHR, H. RICHARD. *The Kingdom of God in America.* Chicago: Willett, Clark & Co., 1937.

HANDY, ROBERT T. "The Religious Depression, 1925-1935," in *Church History,* March, 1960.

Facet Books Already Published

Historical Series:

1. *Were Ancient Heresies Disguised Social Movements?*
   by A. H. M. Jones. 1966
2. *Popular Christianity and the Early Theologians*
   by H. J. Carpenter. 1966
3. *Tithing in the Early Church*
   by Lukas Vischer (translated by Robert C. Schultz).
   1966
4. *Jerusalem and Rome*
   by Hans von Campenhausen and Henry Chadwick.
   1966
5. *The Protestant Quest For A Christian America 1830-
   1930*
   by Robert T. Handy. 1967
6. *The Formation of the American Catholic Minority
   1820-1860*
   by Thomas T. McAvoy. 1967
7. *A Critical Period In American Religion 1875-1900*
   by Arthur M. Schlesinger, Sr. 1967
8. *Images of Religion in America*
   by Jerald C. Brauer. 1967

Biblical Series:

1. *The Significance of the Bible for the Church*
   by Anders Nygren (translated by Carl Rasmussen).
   1963
2. *The Sermon on the Mount*
   by Joachim Jeremias (translated by Norman Perrin).
   1963
3. *The Old Testament in the New*
   by C. H. Dodd. 1963

4. *The Literary Impact of the Authorized Version*
by C. S. Lewis. 1963

5. *The Meaning of Hope*
by C. F. D. Moule. 1963

6. *Biblical Problems and Biblical Preaching*
by C. K. Barrett. 1964

7. *The Genesis Accounts of Creation*
by Claus Westermann (translated by Norman E.
Wagner). 1964

8. *The Lord's Prayer*
by Joachim Jeremias (translated by John Reumann).
1964

9. *Only to the House of Israel? Jesus and the Non-Jews*
by T. W. Manson. 1964

10. *Jesus and the Wilderness Community at Qumran*
by Ethelbert Stauffer (translated by Hans Spalteholz).
1964

11. *Corporate Personality in Ancient Israel*
by H. Wheeler Robinson. 1964

12. *The Sacrifice of Christ*
by C. F. D. Moule. 1964

13. *The Problem of the Historical Jesus*
by Joachim Jeremias (translated by Norman Perrin).
1964

14. *A Primer of Old Testament Text Criticism*
by D. R. Ap-Thomas. 1966

15. *The Bible and the Role of Women*
by Krister Stendahl (translated by Emilie T. Sander).
1966

16. *Introduction to Pharisaism*
by W. D. Davies. 1967

17. *Man and Nature in the New Testament*
by C. F. D. Moule. 1967

18. *The Lord's Supper According to the New Testament*
by Eduard Schweizer (translated by James M.
Davis). 1967

19. *The Psalms: A Form-Critical Introduction*
by Hermann Gunkel (translated by Thomas Horner).
1967

Social Ethics Series:

1. *Our Calling*
   by Einar Billing (translated by Conrad Bergendoff).
   1965
2. *The World Situation*
   by Paul Tillich. 1965
3. *Politics as a Vocation*
   by Max Weber (translated by H. H. Gerth and C.
   Wright Mills). 1965
4. *Christianity in a Divided Europe*
   by Hanns Lilje. 1965
5. *The Bible and Social Ethics*
   by Hendrik Kraemer. 1965
6. *Christ and the New Humanity*
   by C. H. Dodd. 1965
7. *What Christians Stand For in the Secular World*
   by William Temple. 1965
8. *Legal Responsibility and Moral Responsibility*
   by Walter Moberly. 1965
9. *The Divine Command: A New Perspective on Law
   and Gospel*
   by Paul Althaus (translated by Franklin Sherman).
   1966
10. *The Road to Peace*
    by John C. Bennett, Kenneth Johnstone, C. F. von
    Weizsäcker, Michael Wright. 1966
11. *The Idea of a Natural Order: With an Essay on Mod-
    ern Asceticism*
    by V. A. Demant. 1966
12. *Kerygma, Eschatology, and Social Ethics*
    by Amos N. Wilder. 1966
13. *Affluence and the Christian*
    by Hendrik van Oyen (translated by Frank Clarke).
    1966
14. *Luther's Doctrine of the Two Kingdoms*
    by Heinrich Bornkamm (translated by Karl H.
    Hertz). 1966
15. *Christian Decision in the Nuclear Age*
    by T. R. Milford. 1967
16. *Law and Gospel*
    by Werner Elert (translated by Edward H. Schroe-
    der). 1967

Type, 12 on 14 Garamond
Display, Garamond
Paper, White Spring Grove E. F.